Six Stories to Inspire Hope

Written by

Jennifer Wescoe

Illustrated by

Barbara J. Kozero

©2025 by Jennifer Wescoe

All rights reserved. No part of this publication may be reproduced or transmitted in any form or by any means, electronic or mechanical, including photocopying, recording, or any other information storage and retrieval system, without the written permission of the publisher.
Internet addresses given in this book were accurate at the time it went to press.

Printed in the United States of America
Published in Hellertown, PA

Cover and interior design by Leanne Coppola
Illustrations by Barbara J. Kozero

Library of Congress control number available upon request
ISBN: 978-1-952481-86-4 paperback
ISBN: 979-8-89420-030-9 hardcover
ISBN: 978-1-952481-87-1

For more information or to place bulk orders, contact the publisher at Jennifer@BrightCommunications.net.

"The thing to do, it seems to me,
is to prepare yourself so you can
be a rainbow in somebody else's cloud."
~ Maya Angelou

Thank you to the many rainbows in my life. I love you all.

Contents

The Uniquely Wonderful Fish
Featuring Izzy the Fish
page 6

~

The Perfectly Perfect Peacock
Featuring Samuel the Peacock
page 12

~

The Chameleon Who Tried to Blend
Featuring Mellie the Chameleon
page 18

~

The Turtle Who Liked His Routine
Featuring Nelson the Turtle
page 26

The Llama Who Wanted to See the Sunset
Featuring Polo the Llama
page 36

The Hawk Who Nearly Lost Her Voice
Featuring Ava the Hawk
page 46

About the Author and Illustrator
page 63

The Uniquely Wonderful Fish
Featuring Izzy the Fish

There once lived a fish who was unlike any other in the entire great ocean. Her name was Izzy. While the rest of the fish were busy comparing themselves to each other, Izzy would simply do what she loved. She would swim. Swimming was fun. It took her away. It brought her joy.

Whenever Izzy gleefully glided by, everyone watched. Some even stared. Izzy inspired others to find happiness in their own way of swimming. Several fish would often wait for Izzy to pass so they could swim along. On those days, she led them on trips to the ocean's surface, up where the sun kissed their backs and bubbles tickled their bellies.

Izzy was a uniquely wonderful fish.

Although most fish looked forward to Izzy's daily swims, a few didn't want to join her. Perhaps they felt they had better things to do. Perhaps they thought that swimming should be reserved for the hunt. Or perhaps they couldn't understand how the simple act of swimming could bring a fish such delight.

Whenever Izzy crossed their path, the few fish turned their backs. They would tilt their heads slightly to the side and peer at her from the corners of their cold, steel-grey eyes.

One morning, Izzy was on one of her blissful swimming adventures when the few fish decided to play a trick on her. They circled Izzy and asked to come along on her next swim. The few fish heard about the warm sunshine and tickling bubbles, and they wanted to see for themselves if the magical tales the others told them were true.

Izzy excitedly agreed to swim with her new friends. She didn't flap a fin at the possibility that their intentions were anything but honest and good.

Off they went. It wasn't long before the few fish grew tired of swimming with Izzy. They were bored by bubbles that didn't tickle. They couldn't feel the warmth of the sunshine when they swam near the surface.

Right before heading home, the few fish presented Izzy with an idea. They knew of a place on the far side of the ocean that was more splendid than anything she had ever seen. Izzy eagerly listened. She loved to explore and instantly accepted the invitation to join them.

As they swam farther and farther away from the familiar, Izzy began to have second thoughts. The few fish calmed Izzy's fears with words of assurance, reminding her of the marvelous sight she had yet to see.

The few fish swam very fast. Wanting to keep up, Izzy did the same. Soon they were swimming so fast that Izzy could no longer see where she was going.

The water grew murkier. Before Izzy knew it, she was surrounded by the dark and

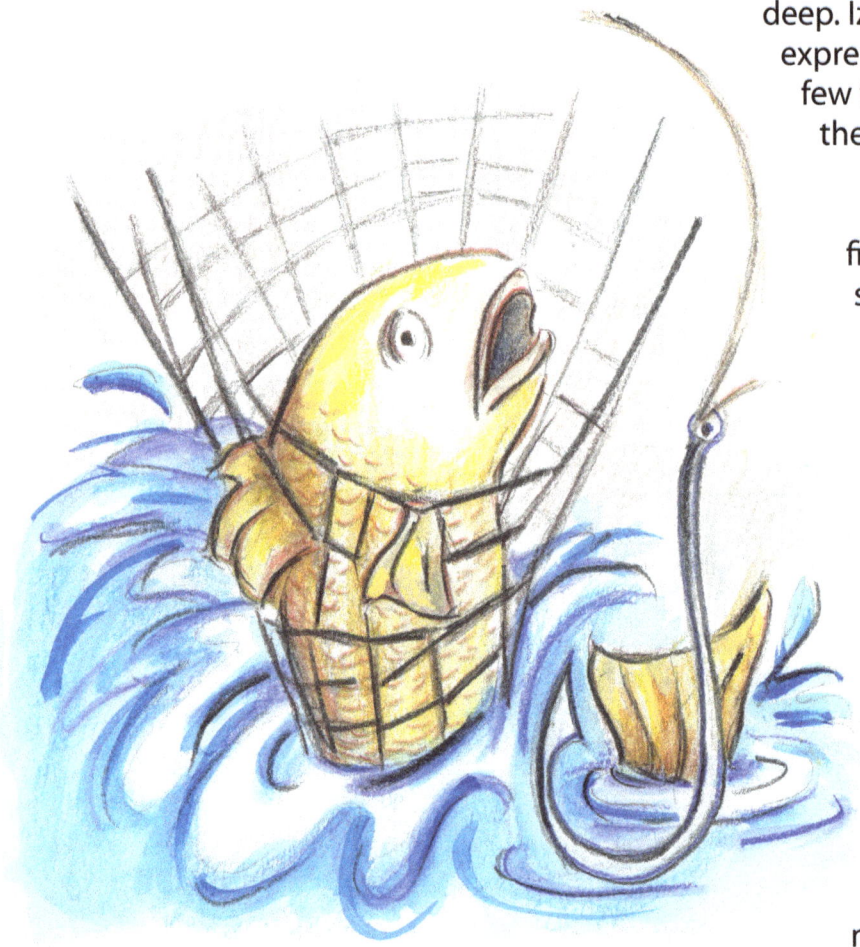

deep. Izzy spun around to express her concern to the few fish, but no one was there.

She was all alone.

The uniquely wonderful fish then did something she had never done before.

She stopped swimming.

Just for a little bit. Just until she could adjust to her new environment.

The water was not only darker, but it was colder—much, much colder than she ever thought water could be. The uniquely wonderful fish then felt something she had never felt before.

Loneliness.

Suddenly, and seemingly out of nowhere, Izzy saw something shiny and glimmery in the distance. She swam closer, hoping to get a better view.

The object was not like anything she had ever seen. It was indeed shiny. It was indeed glimmery. But it was also cold and steely sharp. The object didn't respond to her greetings.

It remained stoic and stubbornly straight.

Izzy had an idea. She could teach her new friend how to swim. They could make it through the dark and deep together!

But when Izzy swam closer, something terrible happened. She felt a strong pulling sensation, dragging her unwillingly and thrashingly to the surface.

Izzy desperately wanted to go back into the ocean, but she could no longer see it.

The brightness of the sun stung Izzy's eyes, and her gills gasped for air. She felt disoriented and confused. The uniquely wonderful fish then felt something she had never felt before.

Pain.

Izzy was soon torn away from the steely object and dropped into a tub of water. She could breathe again. Her eyes adjusted to the light. The uniquely wonderful fish then felt something else she had never felt before.

Relief.

Grateful to have survived, Izzy knew that she must return home at once. But when she tried to swim, her face banged into a clear, hard surface. Izzy was startled, to say the very least. What was this horrible force? The uniquely wonderful fish then encountered something she had never encountered before.

A wall.

No matter how hard Izzy tried to swim, she couldn't move forward. She was trapped.

Izzy watched the ocean in silence as it stretched out in front of her. She could see the sunshine and the bubbles as they playfully splashed with the sparkling waves.

Remembering the stories about those who were taken from the ocean, Izzy shuddered. Nobody ever knew what happened to them. They were never seen or heard from again The uniquely wonderful fish then heard something she had never heard before.

It was the voice of a human.

"We only caught one fish today, but it's a keeper!" boomed the voice. "Yeah, it's in the tank now. We'll make a pretty penny when it goes to market, that's for sure!"

Izzy became embarrassed and filled with regret. Because of her foolishness, she was stuck in a tank. She could no longer do the one thing that made her happy. She could no longer swim.

All she could do was float.

For a while, Izzy did just that.

Float.

Float and sulk.

Izzy also did a great deal of staring. She stared at the sunlight as it danced along the horizon. She stared at the waves as they bravely flowed up to the shoreline, retreating only moments later to rejoin the safety of the tide.

Izzy stared at the invisible walls that seemed to stop her every turn. There had to be a way out. Why couldn't she see it?

Just then, a strange thing happened. She felt something deep inside. It was a bit of a stirring feeling, like a stream of sunlight seeping through her scales.

How was it possible? All smart fish knew the sun didn't shine that way.

But this light was different. It radiated from the inside out. The uniquely wonderful fish then felt something she had never felt before.

Hope.

At this moment, Izzy learned something valuable. It wasn't swimming itself that brought her happiness; it was her desire to swim that gave her the greatest joy of all. It was what made her not only unique but also wonderful.

Learning this lesson gave Izzy strength. It was a strength she never knew existed. Izzy discovered that the walls of the tank weren't blocking her path. They were there to help her see how badly she wanted to be free.

The uniquely wonderful fish mustered up her courage. She gathered all the light she had and always believed she ever would have, and...well, she jumped.

That's right. She jumped!

Izzy jumped higher than the walls of the fish tank. She jumped higher than the ocean waves. She jumped almost as high as the sun itself.

Some might even say that she flew.

Quicker than a splash, Izzy was back in her ocean home. She swam with life, with passion, and with fire! Izzy had a fire inside that could never be extinguished. It was what helped her overcome the darkest depths and rise above the highest walls.

It is the light within that guides us through our most difficult times. This light provides the strength to achieve what others dismiss as impossible.

Izzy still makes trips to the ocean's surface to feel the sunshine on her back and bubbles on her belly. They are reminders to find the good in her day. She has hope in her heart and carries her light wherever she goes.

Because now, the uniquely wonderful fish knows how to truly swim for herself.

The End

The Perfectly Perfect Peacock
Featuring Samuel the Peacock

In a land not too far from here, there once was a magical forest where creatures of all kinds occupied its many trees. And in this forest lived a peacock named Samuel. Everyone admired Samuel for his strength, his kindness, and—of course—his exquisite beauty. The animals even thought he was perfect. They called him, "Samuel, The Perfectly Perfect Peacock."

Samuel cast his eyes downward whenever his friends would call him by this name. He appreciated their kindness, but the praise made him uncomfortable.

"Will you join us for breakfast, sweet Samuel?" asked his peahen friends as they sat beneath the orange tree.

Samuel set his gaze upon the forest. "I'd really love to stay, but I must be on my way. There's just so much to see and do every single day!"

And with that, Samuel was off in a flash. The peahens were barely able to wish him safe travels before he started running. They shook their heads and said, "Now there goes one perfectly perfect peacock!"

Samuel moved among the forest trees, lovingly collecting tasty treasures for his friends to eat and enjoy. He was quite good at foraging, a talent not all peacocks possessed. The insects and berries he found were always a big hit.

Samuel liked to help his friends. He needed to feel useful. He wanted to feel loved.

It wasn't long before Samuel crossed paths with his friend the spotted deer. Samuel had already gathered many plants to give her, and he had just enough time to say hello before heading over to the sweet berry bush. Sweet berries were her favorite snack, and he was the only one who knew where to find them.

The spotted deer jumped and pranced. She gobbled up the treats as soon as Samuel presented them to her. "What's your secret to bringing us the finest food in the forest?" she inquired.

Samuel smiled. "Oh, that I cannot say. I must be on my way. There's just much to see and do every single day!"

And with that, he was off in a flash.

"Samuel is such a busy bird!" said the spotted deer.

In his three years of life, Samuel never failed to miss his daily visit to the forest. He knew exactly how long it took to locate the sweet berries, pick the best ones, and return home before dusk. Samuel ran past his forest friends in a blur, unable to see their smiles and waves. They,

too, wished he would stay awhile to chat and play. Instead, they shrugged and said, "Now there goes one perfectly perfect peacock!"

There was no stopping Samuel. He followed the fork in the path leading to his destination. Samuel was making progress, but he needed to push himself a bit more. He began breathing heavily. "I must be…on my way. I must… be…on my…"

Then something unexpected happened. Suddenly, Samuel's legs felt heavy and slow. "No…this cannot be!" he cried between breaths. "I must…pick the berries…before nightfall!"

But Samuel was too tired to go any further. His body refused to move. Samuel stood motionless, painfully shocked and sad. Tears formed in his eyes.

"What will my friends think if I can no longer bring them food?" he wondered. "What's my purpose?"

Just then, Samuel caught a glimpse of something brilliantly bright. Right there, in the middle of the forest clearing, sat a giant red chair.

Samuel gathered every ounce of his remaining strength and slowly ambled over to the giant red chair. Without a second thought, he plopped right down into it.

The chair was comfortable, yet sturdy. Samuel sighed. He was not used to sitting.

"Hmmm, so this is what stillness feels like." It was an unfamiliar feeling–but not a bad one.

Samuel closed his eyes. He had spent so much time traveling through these very woods, but it seemed that only now he could hear the birds chirping, the frogs hopping, and the rabbits scurrying.

"There are so many sounds here!" he marveled.

Samuel took a deep breath in, and he slowly breathed out. He breathed in again, and he breathed out. Samuel breathed in and then breathed out.

It felt nice to just *be*.

When Samuel opened his eyes, he could see clearer and farther than ever before. He inhaled the invigorating smell of pine tree needles. He wiggled his toes and felt the cool moss beneath his feet.

For the first time, Samuel was at peace.

It felt good.

Samuel liked sitting in the giant red chair. It sure was comfy, but he couldn't sit there forever. He didn't have to. The giant red chair gave Samuel the right amount of support at the right moment, and he was filled with gratitude.

The scenery revitalized Samuel. He took another long look at the forest and reveled in the remarkable view. He noticed a babbling brook in the distance and said, "A cool drink of water is just what I need before returning home."

Samuel rose to his feet. He made sure his balance was steady. Before leaving, Samuel decided to thank the giant red chair for all it taught him. But when he turned around, there was a surprise waiting for him.

A single feather sat upon its seat.

The iridescent turquoise, purple, and royal blue feather glistened in the rays of the sun. Samuel carefully picked up the feather and held it close to his heart. He touched the giant red chair with his wing. "Thank you for your kindness. Whenever I see this feather, I'll remember what you shared with me."

With renewed enthusiasm, Samuel was ready to continue his journey.

Samuel reached the babbling brook. He lowered his head and felt the cool water touch his face. He took a sip. It tasted better than he remembered. Once Samuel quenched his thirst, he lifted his head. Staring back at him was his own reflection.

It was as if Samuel was seeing himself for the first time.

Samuel examined his beak, proud and strong. He peered into his eyes, kind and hopeful. But when Samuel looked beyond his brown and gray feathers, the wonder truly began.

"This fine feather actually belongs to me!" said Samuel as he stared at his own tremendously terrific tail.

The world around Samuel was

beautiful, and he was a part of that beauty!

With a spring in his step, Samuel bounded back to the orange tree to tell his story.

He arrived home to find the peahens and the spotted deer waiting for him. The deer's presence was unusual, but Samuel figured he could recount the tale of the chair and the feather to everyone at once.

Before Samuel could open his beak to speak, the spotted deer spoke first. "We're very glad you're safe, Samuel. We got scared when you didn't make it back before dusk!"

"We missed you, Samuel!" said the peahens.

A feeling of sadness washed over Samuel. In his excitement to return home, he had forgotten to pick berries from the sweet berry bush! What would they think of him for making such a huge mistake?

"I'm sorry to have worried you, and I'm even more sorry because I failed to bring back your favorite treats. I've disappointed you."

Samuel hung his head in shame. "I suppose I'm nowhere close to being the 'Perfectly Perfect Peacock' you think I am."

The spotted deer approached Samuel, nudging his wing with the tip of her nose. "You could never be a disappointment to us. You're so thoughtful and kind," she said. "Samuel, you leave a trail of beauty wherever you go."

"I do?" he asked in genuine disbelief.

"Of course you do!" replied the peahens.

"You don't need to bring treasures for us to love you," said the spotted deer. "You're perfect—perfectly perfect— simply because you're you."

"We love you, Samuel!" added the peahens.

Samuel was profoundly moved by their words. He pulled his shoulders back and held his head high.

Samuel felt taller than the tallest tree in the forest.

From that moment on, Samuel no longer rushed past his friends. He stayed with them, listening and learning about their lives. Instead of bringing the spotted deer sweet berries, Samuel showed her where they grew. He even taught her how to pick the juiciest ones. They walked together—talking, laughing, and prancing some.

The world can move ferociously fast, and it's important to find time for stillness. Because when all is said and done, perfection depends upon perspective.

The End

The Chameleon Who Tried to Blend
Featuring Mellie the Chameleon

Mellie the chameleon greeted the sunrise with a smile on her face and a song in her heart. Each new experience was an opportunity to grow, and she was excited to learn all she could about navigating the world around her.

Life was never dull in the spiny thicket along the desert's edge. Its many inhabitants filled her days with activity. Ever since Mellie hatched, she spent most of her time practicing the art of blending.

Mellie was younger than the other chameleons, and it was hard for her to keep up. But she was definitely up for the challenge. When her friends matched the colors of their environment, Mellie was determined to do the same. She wanted very much to fit in.

The chameleons began their daily practice by visiting the big gray rock. One by one, each of them turned a dusty shade of gray. They seemed to do so with such ease, but Mellie struggled. She felt everyone's stare as they waited to see if she would find success.

Wanting to prove that she could be just like them, she shut her eyes tight and tried to blend.

Finally, the change happened. Mellie opened her eyes and was overjoyed to see that she was the color of the big gray rock. "Hey, everyone! I'm just like you!" Mellie eagerly looked to see if her friends noticed, but they had already moved on.

Mellie felt sad that it took her so long to blend. "Oh, no! They must've gotten impatient with me and left." But Mellie didn't feel down for long. "Next time will be better. I'm sure of it!"

When Mellie caught up with the other chameleons, they were already the color of the red desert sand. They laughed and zoomed along the ground, popping in and out of holes. Mellie had trouble keeping up. "Why does this have to be so difficult?" she wondered. She shut her eyes tight and tried to blend.

After what felt like forever, the change happened. Mellie opened her eyes and was glad to see that she matched the red desert sand. "Okay, I'm just like them." Mellie checked to see if her friends noticed, but they had already moved on.

Mellie needed to prove that she could be just like them.

The chameleons then practiced their skills on the cactus palm tree. It was by far their biggest challenge of the day. The others scrambled up its spiny trunk and effortlessly matched the cactus palm's colors. Mellie struggled, but she refused to give up. She shut her eyes tight and tried to blend.

Eventually, the change happened. Mellie opened her eyes and was relieved to see that she matched the cactus palm. "Phew!" she whispered. "I'm just like them."

Mellie didn't bother to check if the other chameleons noticed her transformation. She knew they were already going back to the spiny thicket. Having worked up an appetite, the chameleons couldn't wait to devour stick bugs and other insects while lounging on the branches.

Mellie wanted to join her friends, but she knew that adapting to the environment was key to her survival. "I bet if I just practice more, I'll blend in no time flat!" she assured herself.

Once the other chameleons finished their meals, they relaxed and played. But not

Mellie. She spent hours attempting to match the colors of her desert home. As soon as it got dark, Mellie crawled into her burrow between the rocks. She wanted to get a good night's sleep so she could wake up bright and early.

The following day, Mellie was up with the sun. The other chameleons continued to rest…but not Mellie. She ate a quick breakfast and launched into her exercises.

The big gray rock was Mellie's first stop. She closed her eyes tight, visualizing its many ridges and cracks. It wasn't easy, but Mellie did it. She matched the big gray rock. "One down. Two more to go!"

Mellie raced over to the red desert sand. Before even closing her eyes, she became the color of the sand beneath her feet. "Alright! I'm on a roll!" she said. "Soon I'll have no problem keeping up with my friends!"

Feeling more sure of herself by the minute, Mellie approached her final test. She stood at the base of the cactus palm tree and looked up. Somehow it seemed taller than before. "Come on, Mellie," she encouraged. "You got this!"

Slowly but surely, Mellie clambered up the cactus palm's trunk. She was terribly thirsty when she reached the top. Mellie leaned over to drink some morning dew from a bend

in the tree. She then spotted something that stopped her right in her tracks. "Woah! The cactus palm is flowering!" It didn't bloom often, so she knew that today was a very special occasion. Mellie was astounded by its beauty.

Once the flower had finished opening, Mellie refocused her attention on blending. She confidently turned the color of the cactus palm almost immediately. "Not too shabby!" she said with a grin.

Mellie hopped down from the cactus palm's trunk. She landed right in time to see striking pinks and purples light up the morning sky. "Could this day get any better?" marveled Mellie.

Little did Mellie realize that she would soon receive an answer to her question.

As Mellie stood watching the sunrise, a single drop of dew silently began to roll down the cactus palm's flower. The dewdrop quickly picked up speed as it traveled down the petals. Before Mellie knew what was happening, the dewdrop landed right on top of her back. It caught the light of the sun and reflected a stunning shower of red, orange, yellow, green, blue, indigo, and violet.

Mellie instantly blended.

She didn't have to try at all.

It was easy.

"Being this colorful feels awesome!" she mused. "I've got to show my friends!"

Mellie was energized in a way she never thought possible. She rushed to the burrows between the rocks so she could share her discovery with the other chameleons. When she arrived home, they were lazily lounging on the branches of the spiny thicket. She scurried over to them, nearly bursting with excitement.

"Hey, everyone! Guess what?!" she exclaimed. "I figured out a new way to blend!"

The other chameleons didn't move a muscle.

Despite their lack of reaction, Mellie continued. "You see, the blooming flower had a dewdrop that created the most magnificent colors!" explained Mellie. "If we hurry, we can catch the rainbow with a few drops to spare!"

"Not now, Mellie," said a chameleon. "We're relaxing!"

"What on earth are you talking about?" yawned another, half listening.

Mellie attempted to reply, "But I think you'd…"

"We don't need to practice anymore today!" interrupted a third chameleon.

"But wouldn't you like to blend with the rainbow?" asked Mellie.

"We're exhausted," said one of the chameleons as he rested his head on a branch." Besides, who ever heard of dewdrops making rainbows, anyway?"

The chameleons shook their heads and continued lounging.

Mellie felt as if her heart had dropped far beneath the desert sand. "Why doesn't my way of blending matter like all the others?" she wondered to herself.

"Mellie, come hang out with us!" said one of the chameleons.

"It's so nice sitting here in the shade!" called another.

"No, thank you," said Mellie in a small voice.

"Suit yourself!" shrugged the third.

Mellie didn't join her friends in the branches. She went back to the cactus palm and rested against its trunk instead. "All I wanted was to bring some sparkle into their lives."

Mellie felt completely deflated. She started to cry. Mellie cried so much that her tears made a puddle on the desert floor. Catching the sunlight, the puddle formed a rainbow of its own.

Once again, Mellie's skin reflected the many vivid colors surrounding her. But this time, she didn't feel happy. "I wish I'd never seen the rainbow that no one else thought was real!"

Mellie couldn't stop thinking about ways to hide her colors. Should she roll around in the mud so they wouldn't show? Could she hide among the shadows for the rest of her life?

Mellie let out a deep sigh. She was different, and she didn't like it at all.

Tears continued to roll down Mellie's face. The sun sank beneath the skyline, and her colors slowly faded away.

Mellie eventually returned home. She retreated into her burrow and cried herself to sleep.

At daybreak, Mellie did not greet the sunrise. She had no smile. There was not a single song in her heart.

When Mellie didn't show up to catch stick bugs with the other chameleons, they noticed.

"Mellie, come join us!" called one of the chameleons into her burrow.

"We miss you!" said another.

"Things are a real drag when you're not around!" added the third.

Mellie ignored them. She feared catching the rainbow and revealing her difference. She worried about what they might think if it happened. Mellie wouldn't take the chance, so she stayed away from the sun. Pretending to sleep was much easier.

A thick fog rolled into the desert, but Mellie couldn't see it. She stayed in her burrow.

The sky grew dark, and it began to rain. At first, only a few drops made their way onto the rocks. But it quickly became a downpour. The rainy season had begun, and the experience was new for all the chameleons living in the spiny thicket.

It rained all day and all night. Mellie remained in her burrow without having the slightest inkling to venture out. Luckily, her home was high enough to avoid flooding.

Mellie thought the rain would never stop. But it did.

After the final raindrop fell, Mellie crawled out from between the rocks. The other chameleons emerged from their burrows, too. The warm sun felt good on their backs.

The chameleons were starving, and food was on everyone's mind. They scavenged the spiny thicket, but Mellie lagged behind.

The group of chameleons traveled to the cactus palm tree in search of a meal. When one of them approached its trunk, he saw something incredible. "Check it out, everyone! The palm's got a flower!"

"Amazing!" said another.

"I've never seen anything like it!" added the third.

Although Mellie had seen the flower bloom once before, its loveliness still impressed her. "I've got to get a better view!" she said as she scrambled up the cactus palm. Mellie reached the top with ease. "The view is even better from up here!"

As if the flower wasn't enough, the chameleons had another surprise in store. When they looked up at Mellie, a rainbow lit up the sky behind her. She instantly blended with its radiant colors. The other chameleons had never seen something so spectacular. They were captivated by Mellie's transformation. "Wow!" was all they could say.

While the chameleons stood in awe, a new spiny thicket inhabitant moved into the area. This dangerous creature was hungry and on the hunt for prey. It was a snake!

The snake slyly slithered up behind the unaware chameleons and noticed their vulnerability. Because the desert sand now reflected the rainbow, her friends no longer matched the environment.

Mellie spotted the snake right away. "My friends, you're in danger!" she shouted.

Without skipping a beat, Mellie jumped onto the ground. She spoke in her calmest voice possible. "Stay completely still. Close your eyes tight, and concentrate on blending."

The other chameleons shut their eyes and set their intention on the task at hand.

"You can do it!" she whispered to them.

The chameleons held their breath.

In an instant, the change happened. Just as the snake was about to strike, the chameleons turned brilliant shades of red, orange, yellow, green, blue, indigo, and violet. The snake could no longer see its food, so it let out a hiss and slunk away in frustration.

Mellie's plan worked! The chameleons were safe!

When everyone was certain that the danger was over, they shifted their attention to Mellie.

"Thank you, Mellie!" they gushed. "You saved the day!"

Mellie shrugged. "Well, I was happy to help."

The chameleons looked up at the rainbow once more before it vanished into the desert sky. Once it departed, they immediately changed back to the color of the red desert sand.

"We're sorry for how we treated you," said one of the chameleons.
"You tried telling us about the rainbow, but we wouldn't listen," said another.
"Knowing how to blend with a rainbow is important, too!" added the third.
"Thank you for apologizing," said Mellie. "I appreciate it more than you will ever know."

From that moment on, the chameleons at the desert's edge viewed life through a different lens. They greeted the sunrise together, each blending in the way they blended best. Mellie stood beneath the cactus palm whenever it bloomed. She knew exactly how to catch the rainbow. The other chameleons took longer to change colors in this vibrant way, and Mellie showed patience with them. She knew that not everyone could turn many shades as easily as she could.

Mellie smiled to herself. She belonged.

Wrapped in her true colors, Mellie the chameleon felt free to be her authentic self. After all, that's the only way to truly live.

The End

The Turtle Who Liked His Routine

Featuring Nelson the Turtle

There's nothing quite like a cool drink of water on a hot summer day. It's what Nelson the turtle looked forward to every morning. He woke up, shrugged the dew off his shell, and made his way over to the slow-moving stream.

After arriving at the water's edge, Nelson leaned over and took a long sip. "Aah, how refreshing!"

Nelson always took his time. He wasn't in a hurry.

Once Nelson quenched his thirst, he walked across the stream on the same sturdy, old oak tree log that had been stuck in the mud for years. He stepped off the log when safely on the other side. Nelson knew precisely where the food was most plentiful, and he dined on a banquet of water lettuce and duckweed every day.

Nelson savored each bite of his breakfast. He allowed his stomach to digest before carefully crossing back over the stream.

Nelson then made his way over to the shoreline to lounge in the warm afternoon sun. Since he had already tried out all the rocks beforehand, the turtle was certain the one he selected was the best for basking.

The day drew to a close, and Nelson slowly walked back to his bed near the shallow part of the stream. He rested in the same spot every night. Nelson was most comfortable sleeping just beneath the surface, with water not even high enough to cover his shell. He avoided anything deeper than he could stand in.

Nelson liked eating what he liked to eat. He liked basking where he liked to bask. He liked resting where he liked to rest.

Nelson liked his routine.

At first daylight, Nelson was already at his usual drinking spot when he froze in place. Nelson heard the sound of something different.

A mallard duck swam up to him. In a lively voice, she said, "Good morning! Good morning! Good morning to you! Today's a fine day, such a fine day! It's our chance to start anew!"

Nelson didn't know what to make of the duck. She spoke louder than any other creature he was used to hearing.

Nelson was rattled. "Excuse me, but I have no time for such pleasantries!" He promptly pulled his head into his shell.

The mallard duck wondered why the turtle hadn't returned her warm welcome. She then tried a different approach. "Hello there! My name is Mother Mallard. What's yours?"

Nelson didn't respond. He pretended not to hear.

"Oh, well," she

said. "He'll come around someday, I suppose."

As Mother Mallard was about to swim away, she heard a faint voice echo from deep within the turtle's shell. "Nelson. My name is Nelson."

Mother Mallard was very happy to hear from him. "It's nice to make your acquaintance, Nelson!"

From that moment on, Mother Mallard knew that she needed to have patience with Nelson. She smiled to herself and went on her merry way.

Nelson waited a long while before cautiously pushing his head out of his shell. He looked left, looked right, and looked left again. Eventually, he settled back into his routine.

As a rule, Nelson kept to himself. He preferred it that way. He didn't want to be bothered by anyone or anything.

Nelson liked to do the same things in the same way all spring, summer, and fall long. When winter arrived, he moved to the rocky shoreline. It was where a turtle could go to get some much-needed peace and quiet.

Before flying south to escape the cold, Mother Mallard spotted Nelson standing on a rock near the water's edge. "See you in the springtime!" she said. "May you stay safe and well!"

Nelson made no reply. He pretended not to hear.

Mother Mallard attempted to shake the chill from her feathers. "Maybe he'll want to be friends when I return." Knowing that she couldn't wait any longer, Mother Mallard gracefully changed direction and flew away.

*****

Winter melted into spring, and Nelson was ready for warmer weather. He yawned and stretched his legs. His throat felt especially dry, and he wanted a drink of water.

After arriving at his favorite spot, Nelson bent his head and took a sip. "Aah, how refreshing! "But when Nelson looked up, he was met with something new.

The sound of splashing water and several tiny giggles disrupted the turtle's solitude.

Nelson was perturbed, to say the least.

Mother Mallard once again swam down the slow-moving stream. But now, six ducklings followed behind. They all greeted Nelson by saying, "Good morning! Good morning! Good morning to you! Today's a fine day, such a fine day! It's our chance to start anew!"

Nelson's eyes widened. He stood stiller than a statue. "I have no time for such pleasantries!" he groused. With that, he abruptly pulled his head into his shell.

The ducklings didn't know what to make of Nelson's behavior.

"Dear ones, Nelson struggles with change," whispered Mother Mallard. "I'm choosing to have patience with him. I hope you can, too."

Taking their mother's lead, the ducklings paid no mind to Nelson's grumblings.

"You've all worked so hard," said Mother Mallard. "Let's take a break from our lessons and have a free swim!"

"Yay!" quacked the ducklings. They splashed and played in the water as Mother Mallard looked on.

Nelson remained in his shell for quite a while. He needed to refocus his thoughts. When he felt ready, he poked his head out of his shell. Looking left, right, and left again, Nelson made his usual trip across the old oak tree log to have breakfast on the other side of the stream.

When Nelson finished eating, he traveled back his usual way and stretched out on his favorite rock. The afternoon sun always had a way of easing his mind. "My nap shall commence right about…" Nelson yawned. "Now."

Nelson was just about to drift off to sleep when he was startled by something new.

The smallest duckling of the group swam up to the riverbank, waddled over to Nelson, and tapped her bill on his shell. "Nelson, would you like to swim with us?" she asked.

Nelson didn't respond. He pretended not to hear.

The duckling didn't waver in her attempts to get the turtle's attention. "Hey, Nelson! You have webbed feet just like me!" She stuck her foot right in his face. "They're perfect for swimming!"

"Swimming??? Swimming?!?" Nelson was taken aback. "I…I have no time for such pleasantries. Now please leave me alone!"

But the little duck continued trying to befriend Nelson. Climbing onto his back, she took a seat right on the top of his shell. "Everyone calls me Tiny Duckling. I may be small in size, but I've got a big personality!"

Nelson's eyes widened. He didn't know what to do.

"Nelson, why don't you ever smile?" asked Tiny Duckling.

"Smiling just isn't… well, it's not part of my

routine," he admitted.

Tiny Duckling was quiet. Nelson grew nervous. He was afraid that he accidentally hurt her feelings.

Several minutes passed in complete silence until Tiny Duckling finally spoke. She tapped Nelson's shell with her wing and said, "It doesn't matter if you smile or not. I'd still like to be your friend."

Nelson couldn't fully comprehend what he just heard. Talking with Tiny Duckling was certainly a new experience, but it was kind of nice. Nelson even felt the beginnings of a smile forming. However, he quickly corrected his mistake and remained expressionless.

You see, Nelson had made a vow to never smile again.

Ever since Nelson was young, he needed a routine. The other turtles would always tease him by saying, "Nelson, you are no fun! " He remembered how they would laugh and walk away.

Nelson's feelings were hurt. Wanting very much to prove that he was fun, Nelson came up with a plan. He decided to throw caution to the wind, skip his daily routine, and throw a party for the turtles.

"We'll be there once we finish our swim!" they promised.

After spending several hours collecting the most delicious plants from far and wide, Nelson was ready to party.

Finally, the moment arrived.

Nelson was barely able to contain his excitement. He waited. And he waited. And he waited some more.

"Maybe they got lost," pondered Nelson. "I wonder if the map I made was clear enough."

Nelson grew tired, but he continued to wait. After the sun disappeared behind the treetops, so did his spirits. None of the turtles showed up–not even one.

Nelson was sad. His face fell into a deep frown.

It was then Nelson promised himself that he would never smile again. Never ever.

Nelson didn't tell his story to Tiny Duckling. He was afraid that she would make fun of him, too.

It was safer to stay silent.

Nelson felt no movement from up above. He didn't know what to think.

With a burst of energy, the tiny duckling stood up and declared, "I will now bask in the sun like my friend, Nelson the Turtle!"

The other ducklings congregated around the pair to see what the fuss was about. Inspired by Tiny Duckling's enthusiasm, they said, "We want to be like Nelson, too!" All six ducklings chose their favorite rock so they could also soak in the sunshine.

Nelson's feet stayed rooted to the ground. He truly was not used to such pleasantries.

After some serious sunbathing, the ducklings jumped into the water and went back to swimming. Nelson saw what a good time they were having.

"Care to join us, Nelson?" asked Tiny Duckling.

Nelson looked at his own webbed feet. He thought about the duck's offer for a moment or two but then reconsidered. "Nope." Nelson shook his head. "No swimming for me."

"That's okay, Nelson," said Tiny Duckling. "See you tomorrow!"

The six siblings formed a line behind Mother Mallard and swam away.

******

As the first beams of sunlight peeked through the trees the following morning, Nelson reached the water's edge. He was shocked to see Mother Mallard and her ducklings already up and swimming. "Good morning! Good morning! Good morning to you! Today's a fine day, such a fine day! It's our chance to start anew!" they sang enthusiastically.

Nelson wanted to wish them a good morning in return, but he lost his nerve. "I have no time for such pleasantries," he mumbled.

Nelson tried to carry on with his routine. But when he set about to cross the stream for breakfast, he was shocked by an unpleasant sight. A trio of frogs sat on the old oak tree log, ribbiting up a storm. They totally blocked his path.

"What's going on here?" he worried. "How will I eat?" Nelson didn't know what to do,

so he retreated into his shell.

The ducklings could see that Nelson was not himself. They rallied around him.

"Are you okay in there, Nelson?" asked Tiny Duckling.

"Leave me alone!" said Nelson as his voice shook.

"Please come out of your shell!" begged Tiny Duckling.

"We're worried about you!" said the other ducklings.

Mother Mallard joined the conversation. "Nelson, I have a question for you. Since my ducklings have become quite good at swimming, why don't we all swim across the stream together?"

"Oh, no! I could never do that! It's not a part of my routine!" said a very nervous Nelson. "Besides, I might sink."

"You won't sink, Nelson!" assured Tiny Duckling. "You have webbed feet like us, remember?"

"Come on, Nelson!" encouraged the other ducklings. "Swim with us!"

Nelson's stomach growled with hunger, but he didn't budge.

"We are your friends, Nelson," said Mother Mallard.

"You can trust us!" chimed in Tiny Duckling.

Nelson timidly brought his head out of his shell. "Very well then," said a reluctant Nelson. "I…I will attempt to swim across the stream with you."

"Alright, let's get to it!" said Tiny Duckling.

The ducklings formed a line behind Mother Mallard. Nelson stepped into the space right between Tiny Duckling and her mother.

Just as Nelson was about to enter the water, he felt a familiar bill on the back of his shell.

"You will swim," whispered Tiny Duckling. "I believe in you."

Nelson was scared, but he kept his composure. He took a deep breath. "Here goes nothing," he said and stepped into the stream.

As he paddled his webbed feet, Nelson kept pace with the other ducks. "I'm swimming?! I'm actually swimming!!" he shouted. The group passed the frogs on the log, but the rude trio looked on without even making one croak of encouragement. After a few more paddles, the swimmers were safely on the other side of the stream.

"Swimming was much faster than walking!" concluded Nelson in amazement.

Nelson felt a smile creeping onto his face, but he stopped it from going any further.

"Nelson, you're a great swimmer!" said Tiny Duckling.

"Why, thank you!" said Nelson as he watched the family of ducks swim away.

Nelson proudly walked over to the water lettuce. By the time he finished eating, the frogs were gone. That meant the log was free and clear. Relieved, Nelson began to walk across the stream. The turtle had just about reached the halfway point when he heard a faint voice call out in the distance. He recognized the sound, and it seemed in distress.

"Help!" cried the small voice. "My foot is stuck! Help! Help!"

The voice belonged to Tiny Duckling. She was in the middle of the stream all alone.

Nelson immediately snapped into action. He jumped into the water and swam toward Tiny Duckling. His webbed feet moved faster than he ever dreamed they could.

When Nelson reached Tiny Duckling, her wings were flailing and flapping about. She bobbed up and then slipped down beneath the water's surface.

"Quick!" he shouted. "Swim over, and get on my back! I will help you!"

"I can't stay afloat, and I don't know why!" shouted the desperate Tiny Duckling. "Help!"

Nelson dipped his head into the water and saw a plastic bag wrapped around her little webbed feet.

Nelson knew that he had to act fast. He held his breath, dove underwater, and scooped Tiny Duckling up onto his shell. "Hang on!" said Nelson.

With Tiny Duckling on his back, Nelson swam until he reached land.

The whole family formed a circle around

Tiny Duckling. Everyone watched as Mother Mallard removed the plastic bag entangling the duckling's feet.

"Phew!" said Nelson. "That was a close one!"

"You saved me, Nelson! Thank you!" said Tiny Duckling. "You're a good friend."

Nelson felt a smile forming along the corners of his mouth. But before it could travel any further, he had a frightening thought. "I've…I've…I've broken my routine!"

Badly shaken, Nelson retreated into his shell.

"Nelson needs a few moments to himself," said Mother Mallard to her ducklings. "In the meantime, let's round up some seeds for dinner."

When Nelson was sure the family had gone, he slowly came out of his shell. He looked left, looked right, and looked left again. Nelson glumly walked back to his bed near the shallow part of the stream and turned in for the evening.

******

On his walk down to the river the following morning, Nelson promised himself that he would have a better day. "Perhaps a cool drink will perk me up." But when Nelson reached the water's edge, he was met with something new.

Mother Mallard and her ducklings were nowhere in sight.

"Oh, no! I must have frightened them away!" he sulked. Nelson stared at the ground. "Nevertheless, I suppose I'll continue on with my routine."

When Nelson approached the old oak tree log, he heard some unwelcome "ribbits."

"Of course, the frogs are back again," he groaned.

But Nelson remembered something before walking away. "Wait a second…I know how to swim!" Without hesitation, Nelson bravely walked into the water and swam across the stream.

As soon as Nelson came ashore, he was greeted by another change. All his favorite foods had already been gathered and neatly arranged. He carefully approached the piles of water lettuce and duckweed. Plenty of seeds and other goodies were assembled as well.

"Hmmm," he said. "I wonder who prepared this fabulous feast."

Mother Mallard and the ducklings slowly moved out from their hiding spots behind the trees.

"Hey there, Nelson!" said Tiny Duckling.

"Hi, Nelson!" acknowledged the others.

"Thank you for your help yesterday," said a grateful Mother Mallard. "To show our appreciation, we wanted to celebrate in your honor."

Nelson surveyed the scene. "You did this….for me?" he asked in a shaky voice.

"We sure did!" answered Tiny Duckling.

"I hope you don't mind us eating with you just this once," said Mother Mallard with an eager look.

Nelson was overcome with happiness. He could no longer hold back.

Nelson smiled the biggest smile in the history of smiles!

Tiny Duckling hopped onto Nelson's shell and said, "Three cheers for Nelson the Turtle!"

"Hip hip hooray! Hip hip hooray! Hip hip hooray!" cheered the ducks in unison.

As it turned out, Nelson *did* have time for such pleasantries. He might even grow to like them.

"It's good to take a break from your routine every so often," said Nelson.

"Absolutely!" agreed Mother Mallard.

Beneath the canopy of trees, Nelson and his friends ate their breakfast together.

"Well, things sure aren't the same today," said Nelson with a smile. "And that's just fine with me!"

The End

The Llama Who Wanted to See the Sunset
Featuring Polo the Llama

Ever since Polo was a young llama, he wanted to have a life full of meaning. Polo spent his days frolicking on the mountainside with his many cousins. He feasted on tasty plants and drank from the lake whenever he needed to quench his thirst.

Polo enjoyed doing many things, but he loved adventures with his father most of all.

"Can we go exploring, Padre?" asked Polo after finishing their grazing session.

"Of course, *mi hijo*!" said Padre with a nod and a wink. "Today is perfect for a quest!"

Padre was the leader of their herd, and he was quite wise. On their daily walks, Polo had plenty of questions to ask his father. He was curious about life's mysteries and wanted to understand all he could about the world.

Padre had many responsibilities, but he always made time for Polo. He gave Polo his complete attention during their walks and was proud of his son's genuine love of learning. Polo's sense of adventure reminded Padre of when he was a young llama with big dreams of his own.

One afternoon, Polo saw a cocoon wrapped tightly against a tree branch. "Padre, what's inside of the cocoon?" he asked.

"That's a good question," replied his father. "A tiny caterpillar lives there. It will go through many changes in its lifetime. But when the moment is right, it will turn into a butterfly that flies all the way to the top of the mountain."

"Woah!" said Polo in awe. He took a couple of steps toward the mountain and looked up to see as far as he could see. Polo was deep in thought until an idea flashed into his mind, ending his silence. "I want to climb to the top, Padre!"

Padre stood right beside Polo and stared at the mountain. "Mi hijo, if you work hard enough and dream big enough, you can accomplish just about anything!"

Polo then fixed his gaze on the sun, and he watched it slowly slide down toward the horizon. Sunsets had particular importance for Polo. Closing his eyes, he felt the warm rays of light tickle his nose. Polo was instantly transported back to when he was a baby cria. He could hear his mother humming as she nuzzled her nose against his.

Polo held this treasured memory close to his heart.

When the warmth faded, Polo opened his eyes. He watched the sun disappear behind the mountain. "I will see the sunset from the mountaintop! I *know* it!"

"All in good time, Polo," said his father. "All in good time."

The pair walked back to the herd. They needed to rest.

"Tuck in time!" called Padre.

The llamas moved to their sleep spots. They formed their bodies into a circle for protection and settled in.

Padre took his usual place near his son and said, "Sweet dreams, mi hijo. Your health and happiness give me strength and purpose. I love you to the sky and back."

Polo rested his head on his father's back. "When I grow up, I want to be just like you." And with that, they both fell fast asleep.

*****

Seasons changed, and the herd grew larger. Although Polo still played with his cousins, he also took on some small responsibilities. Padre watched his son with pride, knowing that he would someday become a great leader.

Early one morning, Padre made an announcement to the herd. "We must seek higher ground where the food is more plentiful."

The llamas nodded their heads in agreement. Once everyone was accounted for, they started their hike up the mountain.

"I bet the sunset will be even more marvelous when we get to our new home!" said Polo eagerly.

He was so excited that he ran ahead of the herd.

"Slow down, Polo!" said his father. "This is not a race. You must learn to enjoy the journey."

Polo doubled back and rejoined the group.

"Onward and upward!" called Padre.

"Onward and upward!" echoed Polo with gusto.

Several hours later, the herd reached their destination. They ate lunch and drank from a cool mountain spring. When the llamas were full, they relaxed and sat in the shade.

"I can't wait to see the sunset from the mountaintop!" said Polo. "When should we leave?"

His cousins had no interest.

"Who wants to go way up there when we have all we need right here?" asked a cousin.

"Not me!" said another.

"Me neither!" added a third.

Polo felt discouraged. He got up and walked over to the spring.

Noticing that his son was alone, Padre joined him. "What's the matter?"

"Nobody wants to go up the mountain with me," said Polo with a frown. "Am I wrong for wanting to see the sunset from the highest height?"

"Dreaming big is important, Polo," said Padre. "But you must understand that not everyone sees things the way you do."

Polo quietly thought about his father's words.

"Hold onto your dreams," encouraged Padre. "They're a part of what makes life worth living."

Over his father's shoulder, Polo could see the sunset. He traveled to a clearing in the trees and absorbed the sun's warm glow. He heard his mother's voice in the wind.

Because they were higher on the mountain, the sun stayed in the sky longer. It still left too soon for Polo. "I bet the sunset will last forever when I reach the top!"

"All in good time, Polo," said Padre. "All in good time."

The pair sauntered back to the herd.

"Tuck in time!" called Padre.

The llamas moved to their sleep spots. Padre sat near his son and said, "Sweet dreams, mi hijo. Your health and happiness give me strength and purpose. I love you to the sky and back."

Polo nestled his head against Padre's shoulder. "Why are there stars in the sky?"

"I'm glad you asked that question," his father replied. "Although I cannot be sure, I believe the stars are a collective of those who have come before us. They support and guide us, so we are never alone. I'm sure they are just as proud of you as I am."

"Thank you, Padre," said Polo. "I love you to the sky and back!" He snuggled up close to his father and fell fast asleep.

*****

At first light, Polo made a decision. "Today is the day I will begin my journey."

Padre chuckled. "I always knew the grass would never grow under your feet, mi hijo!!"

"Will you join me?" asked Polo. "I have so much to learn from you."

Padre considered his son's offer. After some thought, he made his decision. "Yes, I will accompany you."

"Thank you, Padre!" exclaimed Polo. "Thank you!"

The two llamas made their way back to the herd. As Polo was about to bid everyone farewell, his father pulled him aside. "Saying goodbye is permanent. Instead, let's tell them *hasta luego*. It will bring us good luck until we are all together again."

"Okay, Padre!" said Polo.

"Hasta luego!" said father and son in unison. They received a sea of well wishes in return from the other llamas.

The pair smiled at each other. "Onward and upward!"

The air felt cooler as the two llamas hiked up the mountain. They walked through several cloud forests, and a chilly mist surrounded them. The short and curvy trees seemed to watch them pass by.

"Do not fear, mi hijo. A clear sky always lies just above the clouds," assured Padre.

Polo nodded his head, taking in his father's words.

The two llamas hiked a good while longer. Eventually, they took a break to eat, drink, and rest.

Polo had a question for his father. "Padre, how does one learn life's true purpose?"

Padre was amused by his son's curiosity. "That's quite a question!" he replied. "And the answer isn't a simple one."

"Life just seems really complicated, and I don't know why," said a frustrated Polo.

"Well," said Padre, pausing a moment before continuing. "Every day is a gift that brings us new opportunities. That's why they call it the present." Polo tilted his head to the side. "I'm not sure I follow you."

Padre walked over to a patch of dirt. "Perhaps I can show you what I mean." He drew a horizontal line on the ground with his foot. "Many think of time as a straight line that moves forward from here to there."

Polo moved next to his father so he could get a closer look.

"To me, time is more like a circle," said Padre.

Polo paid close attention and watched his father draw a circle on the ground. "As we make our way through life, we each travel along our own circle," he said. "And this circle is in constant motion."

Padre then made a second circle. "Sometimes one circle joins paths with another, and that connection can be magical."

Polo was fascinated.

"Two circles may move together, but no one ever knows how long this alignment will last," said Padre.

"What are you trying to say?" asked Polo.

"We never know how long we have with those we love," said Padre. "That's why we must cherish every moment."

"I think I understand," said Polo. "Can circles meet up again?"

"Of course they can!" said his father. "But nothing is ever certain. That's why being present in our present is the key to living a meaningful life."

After having a good think, Polo came to a conclusion. "I'm so glad our circles have connected!"

"Me too! I love you with my whole heart!" said Padre. "I feel fortunate to have so many wonderful memories with you!"

Father and son exchanged a look. They were better for knowing each other.

Padre's face then became serious. He hesitated, choosing his words carefully. "Mi hijo, I've already seen many sunsets in my lifetime. It's now up to you to complete this part of your journey on your own."

Polo had trouble grasping the gravity of his father's words. "But I have never been alone before. I…I don't know if I'll make it on my own," he stammered.

"You will make it to the top of the mountain, Polo," said his father with conviction. "And when you arrive, please promise to take some time to savor your success. Celebrate your accomplishment before moving on to your next adventure."

Polo fought back tears. "I promise, Padre."

"That's my boy!" said his father with a grin. "I must get back to the herd now. I cannot wait to hear all about your trip when you return."

As Padre turned to go, Polo shouted, "Hasta luego!"

"Hasta luego!" said his father. "Remember your promise, and enjoy every step!"

"I will!" said Polo. "Our circles will reunite again soon!"

They shared one more smile before Padre disappeared into the trees.

Polo faced the mountain. He took a deep breath and continued hiking.

Polo walked as far as he could until day turned to dusk. "By this time tomorrow, I'll have already seen the most amazing sunset ever!"

Once the silvery moon shone in the night sky, Polo knew he needed to rest. He found a comfortable spot to lie down.

"Tuck in time," he announced to himself.

Polo missed hearing his father's voice.

"It's awfully dark out here," he said with a twinge of fear. " Maybe I was a fool to think that I could keep going by myself."

Just then, a gentle breeze brushed across Polo's face. He shivered, but it was not from the cold.

Polo remembered his father's advice. He looked up into the sky, and the evening star captured his attention. He could hear his mother humming in the breeze. Almost as if in a dream, she whispered, "Never fear the darkness. That's when the growth happens."

Polo was not alone, and knowing this gave him great comfort.

"Tomorrow is a big day. I need to be ready." Polo looked up into the sky once more. "Sweet dreams, everyone."

Polo smiled and fell asleep beneath the blanket of stars that knew him and loved him well.

*****

At daybreak, Polo woke up with the sunrise. "Onward and upward!" he shouted as he continued his ascent up the mountain.

Polo trekked higher, and the path grew narrower. The rocks also became sharper. But despite the difficult climb, he kept moving. Polo didn't want to miss the sunset.

All of a sudden, Polo became very dizzy. He needed to stop and rest. "I'm sure I'll feel better soon," he told himself. "And when I do, I'll keep going."

Polo was not prepared for what happened next. Quite unexpectedly, a luminescent trail of sparkling blue light fluttered past. He blinked in surprise. "And now I'm imagining things! I guess I needed the break more than I thought!"

The blue light flew by again. It danced around his head and landed directly on his nose. "Well, hello there!"

Before Polo could respond, the little light flitted away. It touched down on a nearby rock, and a beautiful electric blue butterfly appeared.

"I've come a long way to relay a message," said the blue butterfly.

Polo shook his head in disbelief. Could this be the same creature that was once inside the cocoon at the foot of the mountain? At this point, anything was possible.

The blue butterfly remained focused on its purpose. "You must take care of yourself, Polo."

Polo wondered how the blue butterfly knew his name, but he thought better of asking. Instead, he attempted to explain. "You see, I'm trying to reach the mountaintop before sunset!"

"I understand. But even when you're at your busiest, you still need to think of your health," advised the blue butterfly.

"Now that you mention it," admitted Polo, "I am kind of thirsty."

"You will find a creek and some grass on the other side of this rock," said his fluttery friend. "Please take a few moments to replenish yourself before continuing on your way."

Polo got up and walked around the rock. Sure enough, it was exactly as the blue butterfly had said. He sipped the water, and the small creature landed on his back.

Polo was thankful for the companionship.

As Polo walked over to a green field to eat some grass, the blue butterfly flew off his back and rested on a fern. "Polo, I have one more piece of advice to share with you."

Polo paused his meal.

"You have my full attention."

The blue butterfly flapped its wings in anticipation. Leaning in closely, it said, "When moving forward, you must be aware of all that is around you."

Although Polo couldn't grasp everything the blue butterfly said, he knew he would understand better in time.

Polo turned toward the sun. He was nearing the summit.

When he looked back to bid the blue butterfly farewell, it had already flown away. *"Muchas gracias, mariposa azul!"*

Polo continued to climb. The path was steep, but he had confidence that he would soon reach his goal. "Just a few more steps. Just a few more..."

And then, it happened. Polo arrived at the mountaintop right in time to see the sunset.

The spectacular view took his breath away.

"It's more incredible than I ever imagined!"

Polo was wonderstruck. There were so many mountains–too many to count! Some were covered with jagged rocks, while others were sprinkled with snow. A few were even taller than the one beneath Polo's feet! The setting sun painted everything in soft shades of red and orange. Ancient lakes reflected the colors, silently documenting the entire event.

Polo closed his eyes and felt the warm sunlight tickle his nose. A light breeze blew across his face. Polo thought of his mother and smiled. He felt closer to her now more than ever.

As Polo stood mesmerized, he could hear faint humming in the distance.

The sound soon became more intense. Polo opened his eyes and was astonished at what he saw. He wasn't alone. Other llamas were watching the extraordinary sight right alongside him!

Polo was among those who shared a similar vision.

He joined in their humming, and a peaceful feeling enveloped him.

The setting sun lingered longer than Polo had ever experienced. Together, the llamas watched it dip behind the mountains.

As its final act, all of nature danced as one among dazzling shades of purple and blue. The moon took its place in the night sky. The collective of stars made their presence known, and their luminescence became part of everything it touched.

Polo knew that he had more mountains to climb and sunsets to see. He would soon embark on adventures that would open up his world to infinite possibilities. The past, present, and future are all connected—every moment is now. All we have to do is look up, and our next journey begins.

Even though Polo was excited for what tomorrow had in store, he kept his promise to Padre. He soaked in his success and enjoyed the view. Because having the awareness to appreciate all that surrounds us is the most meaningful present one can ever receive.

The End

The Hawk Who Nearly Lost Her Voice

Featuring Ava the Hawk

If you want to accomplish something great, you've got to have a supportive team by your side. These words echoed in Ava the hawk's mind as she glided through the morning mist in search of breakfast.

Ava loved living atop her lush green mountain home, where the tall pine trees grew as far as her sharp eyes could see. She cherished these moments of serenity before the rest of the world woke up. Ava was an early riser, a hard worker, and a high achiever. She was the first of her four siblings to leave the nest. Ava was talented in many ways, but she excelled most at the art of nest building.

The hawk community was important to Ava. On her daily visits to family and friends, she kept up with the comings and goings of their lives. Ava spent lots of time with the elder hawks. She had much to learn from their life experience and wisdom.

No day ever felt complete without seeing Aunt Penny, one of Ava's favorite hawks. For as long as she could remember, Aunt Penny called to her in the same way.

"Hiya, kiddo!" said Aunt Penny with a smile.

"Hiya, Aunt Penny!" smiled Ava in return.

Ava admired Aunt Penny. Her nests always had a perfect view of the sunrise, and they were stylishly decorated with the finest wildflowers their mountain had to offer.

Watching her aunt sit majestically in a tree that grew beside a waterfall, Ava thought back to when she first ventured out on her own. She needed Aunt Penny's help building her first nest. "Would you mind sharing some of your nest-building skills with me?" asked Ava.

"Stick with me," said Aunt Penny. "I'll teach you how to build one that's the ultimate in comfort, support, and style!"

Ava loved her aunt's upbeat attitude. "Will do, Aunt Penny!"

Aunt Penny was not only terrific at building nests, she was also a wonderful friend. The two hawks spent all afternoon scouting for twigs, sticks, and bark. With diligence and care, Aunt Penny demonstrated the proper techniques to ensure the nest was sturdy and safe. She took Ava under her wing like she was one of her own.

"You've got to prepare your best," said Aunt Penny. "So when the unexpected happens, you can adjust your wings and fly on through it!"

Ava thought about Aunt Penny's advice. "Do you think I'll become an expert nester like you someday?"

"Sure thing!" said Aunt Penny with a twinkle in her eye. "You've got the stuff, kiddo!"

"Thanks, Aunt Penny!" said Ava with a laugh. "You sure know how to boost a gal's spirits!"

Aunt Penny placed the twigs she was carrying inside the nest so they wouldn't fall. "Anything for you."

Ava flew alongside her aunt until she gained enough

confidence to build a nest of her own. "I think I'm ready to make one myself."

"You bet you're ready!" said Aunt Penny. "Fly high, my dear!"

Ava soon became quite good at nest building. She even experimented with new patterns and material combinations. "Everything needs to be just right!" she said as she focused on the details of her latest creation.

Because Ava was absorbed in her work, she didn't realize that another hawk was watching in awe from afar. Ava's imaginative spirit inspired him, but he was nervous to approach her.

After many failed attempts, the hawk finally gathered up his courage and flew over to a nearby tree branch. "Hi! My name is Victor! You rock at making nests!" Hearing his own words, Victor was certain that his awkward approach had failed miserably.

It took a while for Victor's presence to sink in, but Ava was flattered. No one had ever complimented her in this way. She looked up from her project. "Why, thank you, Victor. I'm Ava."

The two hawks didn't know what else to say. They silently gazed at each other for a moment or two.

In an attempt to keep the conversation going, Ava asked, "Would you like to join me on a flight?"

Victor flapped his wings. "Like it?! I'd love it!!"

"Alrighty then!" smiled Ava. "Let's go!"

Ava and Victor's first flying adventure was truly phenomenal. Ava relayed the craft of sturdy nest-building while Victor gave strategies on how to catch the biggest fish in the river. The pair continued to spend time with each other, and it wasn't long before they built their first nest together.

On a treetop overlooking the entire mountain, Ava and Victor found the perfect nesting location. One hawk stacked up twigs and sticks. The other worked on building up its base with moss and bark.

"You know, we make a good team!" said Ava.

"Yeah, we do!" agreed Victor.

Before the two hawks knew it, they finished their nest. They were putting on the final touches when Aunt Penny flew over for a visit. She gave the couple a wreath made of wildflowers. In typical Aunt Penny style, she fashioned it into the shape of a heart.. "May you build many more nests together!"

Ava was blown away by the wreath's beauty. "Oh, Aunt Penny! It's gorgeous!"

"What a thoughtful gift!" added Victor. "Thank you!"

"You're most welcome," said Aunt Penny. "Adding these small personal touches truly make a nest your home."

Ava and Victor gently set the wreath in their nest. They made sure it faced the sunrise. That spring, the couple decided to start a family.

As Ava and Victor prepared for the arrival of their baby chicks, they divided up household responsibilities. One hawk stayed with the eggs to keep them warm. The other brought food to the nest. It was exhausting but energizing work.

Days turned into weeks, and spring became summer. Ava and Victor's anticipation grew with each passing minute. Then, one early summer day, their eggs began to hatch. Victor had just flown in carrying some fresh fish when Ava called him over to the nest. They eagerly watched as four tiny beaks pecked their way out of the shells.

Victor could hardly contain his excitement. "I'm a dad!" he exclaimed. "I'm really a dad!"

"Welcome, precious ones!" beamed Ava. "You were worth the wait!"

Before Ava and Victor could celebrate any further, four expectant faces looked up at their new parents.

"They must be starving," said Ava. "Let's get them fed!"

Ava carefully gave the chicks some food. After finishing, they fell fast asleep. Ava and Victor kept a close eye on their family, but soon the new parents went to sleep, too.

The chicks awoke with the daylight. They were hungry and needed to eat. Ava and Victor got up right along with them.

Victor yawned. "I'm getting the feeling we might need to adjust our schedules a bit now that they've arrived."

Ava looked at him through sleepy eyes. "I think you may be right." She stretched her wings and shook off the morning chill. "How about you find some food while I keep them warm?"

"No problem! I'll be back in two shakes of a tail feather!" Victor flew off, and the search was underway.

*****

As the weeks passed, the family settled into their new routine. Victor provided the meals, and Ava took care of the chicks.

One afternoon, Ava watched Victor disappear into the forest and let out a sigh. She loved being with her family, but the hawk missed having a few moments of her own.

Ava was jolted from her thoughts when she heard a rustling sound from the tree next door. It was Aunt Penny! She had perched on a branch right across from Ava.

"Hiya, kiddo!" said Aunt Penny with a grin.

"Hiya, Aunt Penny!" smiled Ava in return. "What's going on?"

"I figured I'd stop by to check in," she said.

More hawks flew up and landed on neighboring branches.

"Greetings, Ava!" said one of the hawks.

"Howdy, Ava!" said another.

Aunt Penny leaned in and said, "We missed your visits, so we decided to bring the party to you!"

"That's so nice of you all!" said Ava. "But you didn't have to rearrange your day just to see me!"

"Of course we didn't have to," said a hawk. "We wanted to!"

"We've got to lift each other up when we need a boost!" said Aunt Penny. "That's what life's all about!"

Aunt Penny and the other hawks visited every day until the chicks were old enough to explore the world outside of their nest.

*****

The young hawks grew up in the blink of an eye. Before Ava and Victor knew it, the couple set about the task of teaching them to fly. Together, the family practiced how to properly spread and flap their wings. Giggling as they traveled from one low tree branch to another, the young hawks flew higher and higher each session.

Aunt Penny and her friends sat on nearby branches to show their support.

"Come on!" encouraged Ava.

"Keep it up!" coached Victor.

One by one, each of the young hawks took flight.

"Look everyone, one of our babies is flying!" said Ava. "She shines like the sun! Let's name her Lina!"

"There goes another!" said Victor. "He flies with such purpose. We'll call him Arman!"

Ava watched the third young hawk fly with ease. "What a strong little guy! His name will be Milo!"

The fourth young hawk, the smallest of the group, patiently waited for his chance. He looked to his parents for approval. They waved their wings in excitement. He nodded his head, faced the open sky, and took off without a hitch.

"That one's got a heart of gold!" said Victor. "We'll name him Koda!"

Everyone breathlessly watched the young hawks fly through the air with pure delight.

"I've never been happier in my whole life!" said Ava.

"Neither have I!" said Victor. "Look at them go!"

"We make a great team!" said Ava.

"We really do!" agreed Victor.

The hawks in attendance chirped with glee. It was a wondrous moment for the whole community.

After flying lessons, the young hawks learned how to hunt and build nests. Victor gave fishing lessons, and Ava introduced them to nest building.

Under Ava's skillful direction, the young hawks made their first nest. "You've got to prepare your best," she instructed. "So when the unexpected happens, you can adjust your wings and fly on through it!"

Aunt Penny flew by and checked out the finished product. "Nice work!"

"Thanks, Aunt Penny!" called the young hawks.

Aunt Penny circled back to the nest and flew up right beside Ava. "You've got the stuff, and don't you ever forget it!"

Ava was grateful for Aunt Penny's support.

When Victor brought up the idea of taking the young hawks to the river so they could learn how to catch fish, Ava had concerns. The river was right at the forest's edge, and it would mean flying their farthest trip yet.

Victor put his wing over his heart. "I promise to be extra vigilant."

Ava did her best to shake off her hesitation. "I'll stay here and serve as lookout. If you need me, I'm only a call away."

"Fantastic idea!" said Victor.

As her family was about to leave, Ava couldn't resist adding one final piece of advice. "Please be careful!"

"I will!" assured Victor. "You can count on me!"

Ava acknowledged him with a final nod. She shook her feathers and flew up to the top of their tree.

Victor turned to his offspring and said, "Come on, kids! Let's have ourselves an adventure!"

The young hawks squealed with excitement. They lined up in their designated take-off locations, flapped their wings, and traveled toward the river.

Ava was on full alert as she scanned the entire mountainside. Her family needed her, and she was not going to let them down.

Once Ava inspected every inch of the woods, she tried to relax. She breathed deeply and took in the tranquility of her surroundings. Listening to the wind in the trees calmed her. "It sure is peaceful up here."

Without warning, Ava heard a sharp, screeching noise. She bolted upright. Her feathers stood on end. The ear-piercing sound emanated from a place close to her family's fishing location. Ava turned her head just in time to witness a large pine tree topple over. It landed with a loud crash.

A few seconds passed, and the screeching started again. Two more trees fell. Ava then spotted a yellow machine with a large saw attached to its front. It trudged loudly through the mud where a group of trees used to live. She kept a close eye on the machine until it drove away, but the threat was far from over.

Ava called out to Victor. She listened for his familiar reply. Hearing nothing in return, she called him again. Over and over, Ava continued to call Victor. But only the sound of her voice echoed back, empty and unheard.

Horrified, Ava feared that her family was in danger.

The eerie stillness made Ava extremely uncomfortable. She tried to explain away Victor's lack of response. "Perhaps he's too far away and can't hear me."

When Ava attempted another round of calls, something shocking happened. A small, hoarse sound squeaked out. "What's wrong with my voice? "Trying her call again, she struggled to make even a quiet cry.

Ava felt powerless. She could only watch, wait, and hope that her family would somehow return home.

Suddenly, Ava noticed a tiny figure emerge from a clearing in the woods. Then, four more appeared. The figures grew larger. It was Victor flying with their four young hawks!

Ava was relieved beyond measure when her family landed safely in their tree.

"Phew, that was a close one!" said Victor. "I was scooping up a fish from the river when a gigantic tree came out of nowhere and almost fell on me! I somehow maneuvered around it, but I dropped our dinner." He lowered his eyes. "I'm sorry."

Eating was the farthest thing from Ava's mind. "Well, what's most important is that no one's hurt."

Victor tilted his head. "Ava, are you okay? I can barely hear you."

"I'm fine. I just need to rest my voice," said Ava, not completely believing her own words.

"I think we all could all use some rest," admitted Victor.

The young hawks were so tired that they fell asleep without wanting dinner. It wasn't long until Victor followed them into slumber. While the rest of the family slept, Ava's thoughts kept her awake the entire night.

Ava quietly woke Victor up at daybreak. "Let's go somewhere and talk in private," she whispered. Without a word, he followed her to another tree.

Ava cleared her throat. "The forest is in danger. We need to do something—and fast."

"Yes, we do," he acknowledged. "And how can we warn the others?"

The two hawks sat in silence, both preoccupied with their own thoughts.

Ava had an idea. "Let's meet as a group."

"Good thinking!" said Victor. "And we'll all come up with a game plan together!"

Ava suddenly became worried. "But what about my voice?"

"With some rest, I'm sure it'll be back and better than ever!" he assured.

As the sun rose, the family ate a quick breakfast. They decided to inform the other hawks about the meeting. Aunt Penny's place was their first stop.

Their aunt listened closely as Victor relayed the story of the yellow machine. "I was afraid something like this would happen again. I'll talk with my friends, and we'll spread the word about the meeting."

"Thanks, Aunt Penny," said Victor.

"You got it!" she confirmed.

"We want to help, too!" said all four young hawks in unison.

"Of course, we'll all pitch in and play our part," said Victor. "Now let's get to work!"

Victor and the young hawks took off into the sky.

Before Aunt Penny left, she flew to the tree branch beside Ava. "Please promise me that you'll rest up for tonight. We need you in tip-top shape!"

Ava reluctantly nodded her head in agreement. "I promise."

"Good!" said Aunt Penny.

Ava was worried. "What if I can't get through to the other hawks?"

"Sometimes leadership is knowing when to share the load," said Aunt Penny.

"Easier said than done," admitted Ava.

Aunt Penny looked out at trees, deep in thought. "I understand. Trust me, I do."

Ava anxiously waited for her aunt to continue.

"See that tree across the way?" Aunt Penny pointed forward with her wing. "It's the tall one with more branches than a hawk can count."

Ava spotted a beautifully full tree across the way. "Yes, I see it."

"A tree that solid doesn't just pop up overnight," said Aunt Penny. "It put a lot of work and energy into grounding itself with deep roots. That's why it's able to support so much life."

Ava struggled to make the connection. "True, but how does the tree's story relate to mine?"

"You've got to be patient with yourself," said Aunt Penny. "Others will see your positive intention, and they'll want to help, too."

"Thanks, Aunt Penny," said Ava.

"Anytime!" replied Aunt Penny. "And when I say that you've got the stuff, I mean it!"

Ava watched Aunt Penny fly away until she became a dot on the horizon. She followed her aunt's advice and took a nap.

Once the sun sank behind the trees, the hawks gathered. The meeting attendees sat on neighboring branches and formed a circle.

"What a turnout!" said Victor. "Only two families declined the invitation. They said they were too busy to participate."

"Let's focus on those who are here," said Ava.

Ava felt better and her voice sounded stronger. She called the meeting to order. "Good evening, everyone. We've assembled here tonight to express concerns about our community's safety."

Victor was the first to speak. He told his story about the falling tree. When he finished, others contributed to the discussion with harrowing tales of their own. They listened intently with the understanding that everyone needed to feel heard. Once the hawks expressed their concerns, they moved to generate a course of action.

"What can we do to protect each other and ourselves?" asked Victor.

A hawk spoke up from across the circle. "The other side of the mountain has many trees, plenty of food, and lots of space. It's quite the journey, though."

They all reflected on the weight of her words.

Ava broke the silence. "Who's in favor of going over the mountain?"

The hawks paused before responding, knowing their decision would surely change their lives. After some time, one hawk looked around the circle and boldly raised his wing. It wasn't long before the other hawks raised one as well. Leaving their homes wouldn't be easy, but it was necessary.

"It's unanimous. The hawks have spoken, and we will make our move," concluded Ava. "Now how will we do it?"

Victor made the first suggestion. "I'll fly with a group of hawks to the sanctuary, and we'll work in shifts building nests."

"Super idea. Who will go with him?" asked Ava.

Several hawks raised their wings and volunteered their services.

Lina spoke on behalf of her siblings. "We can stockpile nest-building materials."

"I'll join the young ones on their search!" said Aunt Penny. "Who's with me?"

Aunt Penny's friends raised their wings.

"I'd be glad to assist those still learning to fly!" offered a hawk.

"And I'll help them hone their hunting skills!" added another.

"But who will oversee the operation?" asked Victor.

"I nominate Ava," replied an elder. "Who agrees?"

The hawks unanimously raised their wings in support.

Aunt Penny turned her attention toward Ava. "Do you accept this nomination?"

Ava was honored and felt a strong sense of duty. "I do."

"Then it's settled," said Victor. "Ava will lead us to safety."

"We begin at dawn," said Ava. "I will keep a close watch for signs of danger. Some of us will build nests. Others will perch on treetops and call out open travel routes. When we act as one voice, our team will send a message that resonates far and wide."

Once everyone chose their role, Ava adjourned the meeting.

A hawk flew up to Ava before leaving. She wanted to express her gratitude. "Thank you. You helped me to understand that I'm not alone."

"You're welcome," said Ava. "We'll get through this together."

"Yes, we will!" said the hawk and flew away.

Aunt Penny landed on a tree branch beside her. "You're doing a great job, kiddo!"

"Thanks, Aunt Penny," she said. "I'm lucky to have you in my life."

"I'd say we're all lucky to have each other," concluded her aunt.

Ava and Aunt Penny flew into the evening twilight side by side.

*****

The hawks woke up at first light. Unified in their purpose, everyone took their positions and got to work. They concentrated on the task at hand. They adapted their plan if an issue popped up. They were in flow, and it was a sight to behold.

Over the next several mornings, the hawks kept building until they reached their goal. They made nests for the entire community in only five days!

Ava settled onto a tree branch to rest for the night. When they needed to leave, they'd be ready.

Unfortunately, the hawks didn't have long to wait.

An ear-piercing screech abruptly jarred Ava from her slumber. It was louder and harsher than any sound she had ever heard before. As she peered through the tree branches, a seemingly endless line of yellow, steely-sawed machines positioned themselves along the foot of the mountain.

Ava flew over to Victor. "Wake up! They've come to take the trees!"

Victor was immediately alert. "I'll take the kids to our new nest. We haven't flown the entire route yet, but I'm sure they'll be fine."

"I hope so!" said Ava with concern.

"Will you come with us?" asked Victor. "The longer you wait, the more dangerous it will become."

"No, I must warn everyone," she said. "I'll meet you on the other side of the mountain."

Tears glistened in the corners of Victor's eyes. "Alright then, I'll see you soon!"

The pair snapped into action. Victor woke up the young hawks, and Ava moved to her treetop post.

Ava was about to sound the alarm when she remembered how it felt to be voiceless. "Stay strong!" she reminded herself.

Taking a deep breath, Ava channeled her energy and let out a warning call loud enough to wake up the entire forest.

Ava's voice was back, and it sounded better than ever.

The hawks acted quickly. They flapped their wings in rhythm and flew like instruments in a symphony. No one was left behind.

As Ava assessed the situation, two hawks confronted her.

"What do we do?" one asked with desperation. "Our families didn't go to the meeting, so we didn't build any nests!"

"We made extra ones. Fly with the others, and they'll show you where to go!" directed Ava.

"Thank you!" said the appreciative hawks. They swiftly flew away.

Within seconds, the yellow machines rolled forward and began destroying their home.

Ava took one final look at the forest and let out a screech of her own. She flew with ferocity into the sky, never wavering in the belief that her journey would be successful.

Clouds enveloped Ava as she soared high above the trees. The air felt cool and crisp.

When Ava reached the other side of the mountain, she flew in the direction of her family's nest. She watched Victor's features take shape. However, no other figures came into view. He sat on a tree branch by himself.

"Ava, I'm so glad you're okay!" said Victor as soon as she reached the tree. "But the rest of us aren't here yet."

"What happened?" she asked fearfully.

Victor frowned. "We got separated."

Ava sat beside Victor and comforted him with her wing. "They'll be here soon. Until then, we wait."

The two hawks scanned the skyline for any trace of their family. With each passing minute, they grew more and more uneasy.

All of a sudden, they detected movement in the distance.

"I think it's them!" said Ava.

"So do I!" agreed Victor. "But it's tough to see anything through the clouds."

Ava took a deep breath, summoned her strength, and called out to her family. Her voice sounded loud and clear despite the hazy air.

Hearing their mother's familiar call, the far-off figures altered their course.

Lina, Arman, Milo, and Koda flew toward their tree.

"It's them! They heard you, Ava!" said an ecstatic Victor.

Ava was filled with joy! Her family was safe!

"They're flying with another hawk!" observed Victor. "Who's with them? I can't quite tell."

The sky cleared to reveal that the young hawks were accompanied by none other than their Aunt Penny.

Ava and Victor chirped with happiness as their family landed on several surrounding branches.

"You kids must be starving! I'm going down to the river to catch the biggest fish you've ever seen!" announced Victor. "Tonight, we celebrate!"

Everyone cheered.

Aunt Penny landed on the closest tree branch. She was worn out from the long trip.

"You're a lifesaver, Aunt Penny!" said Victor. "I'm bringing you back dinner, too!"

"That sounds lovely," said their weary aunt.

Victor nodded his head and flew off.

Now that her family was accounted for, Ava felt she could finally breathe freely again. "How can I ever repay you?"

"Well, having you all as my family is payment enough," said Aunt Penny. "One of the most rewarding parts of life is helping others find their voice once you've found your own."

Ava understood the meaning behind Aunt Penny's words. "Thank you for being there for us."

"Always and forever!" said Aunt Penny with a grin. With that, she flew to her tree for some rest.

*****

The sky eventually cleared, and Victor returned to the tree with food. "Dinner is served!"

Everyone took the party to Aunt Penny's place.

"Wow!" said Aunt Penny. "This meal is fit for a queen!"

"You deserve that and more!" said Ava with deep sincerity.

"We brought you a present, Aunt Penny!" said Arman.

"Thanks for helping us fly over the mountain!" said Lina.

"We spent the whole afternoon putting it together for you!" said Milo proudly.

The four young hawks held up a heart-shaped wreath made of mountain wildflowers.

Koda placed his wing over his heart. "We made it with love!"

"How stunning!" said a deeply moved Aunt Penny. "Thank you so much!"

Ava remembered her aunt's advice about nest-building. "Because adding these small personal touches…"

"… truly make a nest your home," finished the four young hawks.

"We love you, Aunt Penny!" said Ava.

"I love you, too," she said.

The family said their goodbyes and went back to their tree.

"We really do make a great team!" said Ava.

"We sure do!" agreed Victor.

"We certainly do!" declared the young hawks.

After everyone else had gone to sleep, Ava flew to the tallest treetop she could find and reflected on her day. Calling out to her new mountain home, a clear and confident sound echoed back. "It's nice to feel like you're a part of something bigger."

Ava the hawk had finally found her voice. It was there all along, just waiting to be discovered. And now that she knew its value, she vowed to always keep it safe and strong.

The End

...or perhaps...

The Beginning

About the Author

The art of storytelling has played an integral role in Jennifer Wescoe's life for as long as she can remember. Whether taking the form of written or spoken word, she loves getting lost in the lives of characters. Some of her favorite childhood memories include trips to the library with her mother and sister. Excitedly wading through piles of books, Jennifer loved learning about different times, places, and perspectives. She credits many amazing teachers for inspiring her imagination and encouraging her creativity. Jennifer's first book, *The Magic Shoes*, was published after winning the Bethlehem Public Library's "Write Your Own Book" contest when she was in third grade.

A native of Pennsylvania, Jennifer received both her undergraduate and graduate degrees from Lehigh University. She has served as an English, Theatre Arts, and Gifted Seminar educator for over twenty-five years. Jennifer is passionate about helping learners of all ages find their voice through reading, writing, creating, and performing. As director of the Freedom High School Theatre Company, she was featured in the documentary *Most Valuable Players* and appeared on the Oprah Winfrey Network. Jennifer and her students were also the subject of the WB's web series *High Drama 2: Against All Oz*. When Jennifer is not in the classroom, you can find her singing a tune, walking among the trees, and enjoying the company of her family, friends, and little dog Theo.

About the Illustrator

Barbara Kozero's dual passions for art and education have guided her professional career. Her artistic interests began as a child, when she started sketching pictures of mice and cats in school notebooks. Since then, she has produced a whimsical and unique body of work including mosaic reliefs, fanciful clocks, and a series of "imagination drawings." For nineteen years, she worked as an art educator for elementary and middle schoolers, instilling in them the same love for unique expression that has been so important in her life. She has also enjoyed the opportunity to combine her artistic and educational callings as the author and illustrator of *Finding the Magic in Me*, a magical story she wrote for her granddaughter. Barbara is delighted to illustrate Six Stories to Inspire Hope for her good friend and fellow educator Jennifer Wescoe. She hopes that her drawings will help bring Jennifer's story to life in the minds of readers and encourage them to embrace who they are.

"Life's like a movie, write your own ending.
Keep believing, keep pretending.
We've done just what we set out to do.
Thanks to the lovers, the dreamers, and you."
—Kermit and the Muppets

www.ingramcontent.com/pod-product-compliance
Lightning Source LLC
Chambersburg PA
CBHW061352010526
44107CB00011B/913